ideals COUNTRY

More Than 50 Years of Celebrating Life's Most Treasured Moments

Vol. 52, No. 4

"How softly runs the afternoon
Beneath the billowy clouds of June!"

—Charles Hanson Towne

IDEALS—Vol. 52, No. 4 June MCMXCV IDEALS (ISSN 0019-137X) is published eight times a year: February, March, May, June, August, September, November, December by IDEALS PUBLICATIONS INCORPORATED, 535 Metroplex Drive, Suite 250, Nashville, TN 37211. Second-class postage paid at Nashville, Tennessee, and additional mailing offices. Copyright © MCMXCV by IDEALS PUBLICATIONS INCORPORATED. POSTMASTER: Send address changes to Ideals, PO Box 148000, Nashville, TN 37214-8000. All rights reserved. Title IDEALS registered U.S. Patent Office.

SINGLE ISSUE—U.S. $4.95 USD; Higher in Canada
ONE-YEAR SUBSCRIPTION—8 issues—U.S. $19.95 USD; Canada $36.00 CDN (incl. GST and shipping); Foreign $25.95 USD
TWO-YEAR SUBSCRIPTION—16 issues—U.S. $35.95 USD; Canada $66.50 CDN (incl. GST and shipping); Foreign $47.95 USD

Printed and bound in USA by The Banta Company, Menasha, Wisconsin. Printed on Weyerhaeuser Husky.

The paper used in this publication meets the minimum requirements of
American National Standard for Information Sciences—Permanence of Paper for Printed Library Materials, ANSI Z39.48-1984.

Unsolicited manuscripts will not be returned without a self-addressed, stamped envelope.

ISBN 0-8249-1128-8   GST 131903775

Cover Photo ORGAN PIPE CACTUS NATIONAL MONUMENT. Arizona. Ed Cooper/H. Armstrong Roberts.

Inside Front Cover SUMMER SAILING. Eleanor Lane, artist,
under license of InterArt Licensing.

Inside Back Cover WILDERNESS SPIRIT. Lynn Kaatz, artist,
under license of InterArt Licensing.

Hideaway

Willena Burton

Deep in the woods
Where the violet hides
And the night owl stirs in his sleep,
There's a rotten log
Where moss abides
And cottontails play hide-and-seek;
From a crack in the sky
A bright sunbeam falls,
Startling a young cricket's dream,
And he creaks out his song
From a leafy wall
As he warms his legs in its beam.

Deep in the woods
A doe and her fawn
Step softly on silent grass.
And they stoop to drink
From the fountain splash,
A pause—and then they pass.
From canopied shadows
The waterfall sings
As it rushes along with the stream—
A symphony played
In gossamer green
Of places to hide and to dream.

HIDEAWAY
Mt. Hood National Forest, Oregon
Steve Terrill Photography

TIGER SWALLOWTAIL ON HYDRANGEA BLOOM. Portland, Oregon. Steve Terrill Photography.

Butterfly

Vilet Bennett

Light, bright,
   Flitting, merry—
Dear, delightful,
   Dancing fairy—
Flower to flower,
   Here, there, gone—
Golden butterfly
   Across the lawn.

ENDANGERED KARNER BLUE, *Lycaeides melissa samuelis*. Michigan. Larry West/FPG.

Blue Beauty

Grace Tall

Did some violet,
    Wanting flight,
Pull its roots up
    One fair night
And, spurning all
    Terrestrial things,
Convert its petals
    Into wings
Then, aiming for
    The fields of sky,
Take off—
    An azure butterfly?

Little Hummingbird

Lorene Everingham

Little bird with the whirling wing,
  Have you no happy song to sing?
You quickly flit from flower to flower
  To gather nectar in sun and shower.
Your tiny wings look very sheer;
  For gossamer they now appear
While daintily you seem to sup
  From every upturned petal cup.

Lovely in color and design,
  The settings where you daily dine—
A wee drop here, a wee taste there
  From blooms that set a table fair.

Deep-sheltered sweetness God preferred
  To give His little hummingbird,
Who darts so swiftly, not to miss
  A chance to give each flower a kiss.

Flashing and twirling to and fro,
  Back and forth I saw you go.
You did not sing a happy song,
  And yet your trust in God was strong.
O little bird with the humming wing,
  Today you caused my heart to sing.
I did not drink from the flowerlet cup,
  And yet my soul was lifted up.

WILD GARDEN HUMMINGBIRD
Susan Bourdet, artist
Courtesy of the artist and Wild Wings Inc.
Lake City, Minnesota

Along a Summer's Path

Lon Myruski

I strolled along a summer's path
　　Enswathed in fragrant air
And marveled at the wonders wrought
　　Through Mother Nature's care.
The path wound over hill and dale
　　To lend a sweeping view
Then crossed a shady glen to keep
　　Its millstream rendezvous.

I paused along a summer's path
　　Beside a crystal stream
Where cloud bouquets were mirrored in
　　A most engaging scene.
And on the water whirligigs
　　Reeled round in promenade
While songbirds trilled so sweetly with
　　Their summer's accolade.

I stopped along a summer's path
　　Deep in a piny wood
And listened to the chatter in
　　A chipmunk's neighborhood.
Then in a beat my heart composed
　　This sentimental line
That etched itself upon my soul:
　　I love the summertime.

BLANCHARD BROOK TRAIL
White Mountain National Forest
Pinkham Notch, New Hampshire
William Johnson
Johnson's Photography

The Country Schoolhouse in Summer

John C. Bonser

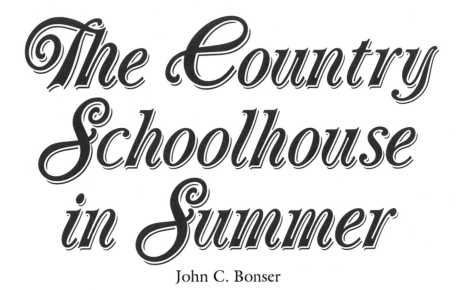

The countryside, in greens and golds,
Reflects the warmth of Summer's smile.
And I, freed from my chores this morn,
Walk down the road a dusty mile

To where a weathered schoolhouse stands,
Half-hidden by tow'ring trees of oak.
And silence reigns, save from a pond
Nearby I hear a bullfrog croak.

I gaze within on empty rooms,
The blackboards bare, the chairs in place.

How strange to see no bobbing heads,
No upraised hands or puzzled face

Or hear, from darkened hallways, sounds
Of students running out to play!
Like them, in summers long ago,
I too was glad to stay away.

But now could I bring back the past,
Its time-hinged doors swing open wide,
With eager steps a wiser boy
Would joyfully slip back inside!

Strawberry Dreams

Eva Mahanna

The call to wake seemed far, far away;
Unmistakably a dream, I wished, but I knew.
Dawn tugged and pulled at heavy eyelids;
The fog quickly lifted as warm feet met cold floor.

A biscuit after dressing, I, crate of small boxes in hand,
Set out to fulfill morning's mission.
A quarter-mile hike, a checkerboard
Of green thickly dotted with red,
And an easy smile came to my face.
"This won't take long," I told myself.

First box half full in only a minute.
No sense rushing, I reasoned.
Could berries taste as good as those look?
I had to know.
So I knelt for a sample, just one,
Then sat for ten more.
Like a fine morning mist, my purpose
Suddenly evaporated.

An hour later, I, stretched out between rows,
Not a ripe berry nearby,
Could be found with one half-full box
Surrounded by empties.
Consciousness faded as a fat, woolly worm
Marched across a leaf;
And the call to wake seemed far, far away.

Opposite Page. RIPE STRAWBERRIES. Superstock.

Family Recipes

Favorite Recipes from the Ideals Family of Readers

Editor's Note: Please send us your best-loved recipes! Mail a typed copy of the recipe along with your name, address, and telephone number to Ideals magazine, ATTN: Recipes, 535 Metroplex Drive, Suite 250, Nashville, Tennessee 37211. We will pay $10 for each recipe used. Recipes cannot be returned.

RHUBARB DESSERT

Preheat oven to 350° F. In a medium mixing bowl, stir together 2 cups flour and 2 tabl[e]spoons granulated sugar; with a pastry blender, cut in 1 cup butter or margarine until th[e] mixture is crumbly. Press the mixture into the bottom of a 9- x 13- x 2-inch pan. Bake [ ] minutes.

In a large mixing bowl, combine 5 cups chopped rhubarb, 6 beaten egg yolks (reser[v]ing the whites), 2 cups granulated sugar, 4 tablespoons flour, 2 tablespoons cornstarch, [ ] cup half-and-half, and ¼ teaspoon salt; mix well. Pour over the base and bake 45 minute[s.]

In a mixing bowl, beat the 6 reserved egg whites until foamy; gradually add ¾ c[up] granulated sugar and beat until stiff peaks form. Spread meringue over the rhubarb mi[x]ture. Bake 10 minutes. Serve within 24 hours.

Elsie Tschabuschnig
Swan River, Manitoba

MOTHER'S HUCKLEBERRY SOUP

nse well 1 cup fresh huckleberries (or blueberries). In a medium saucepan, combine the rries with 2 cups water and ½ teaspoon cinnamon; bring to a boil. Reduce heat and simmer minutes. Gradually add ⅓ cup granulated sugar, stirring until thickened.

If the soup needs additional thickening, combine 1 tablespoon cornstarch with 2 tablepons water; mix well and gradually stir into the soup. Cook over medium heat, stirring until e soup is clear. Remove from heat and chill for at least 1 hour before serving. Garnish with mon slices, sour cream, and nutmeg before serving in chilled bowls. Makes four servings.

Linda Hutton
Decatur, Illinois

FRESH PEAR PIE

eheat oven to 400° F. In a large mixing bowl, combine 4 cups peeled and diced pears (about medium pears), ⅓ cup granulated sugar, 1½ tablespoons quick-cooking tapioca, 1 tablepon lemon juice, and a pinch of salt; mix well. Set aside for 10 minutes.

In a medium mixing bowl, stir together ¼ cup flour, ¼ cup packed brown sugar, ¼ cup rnflake crumbs, 1 cup ground pecans, and ½ teaspoon cinnamon. With a pastry blender, cut 4 tablespoons butter or margarine until the mixture is crumbly. Sprinkle 1 cup of crumbly ixture in the bottom of an unbaked 9-inch pastry shell; top with pear mixture. Sprinkle maining crumbly mixture on top. Bake on lower rack for 30 to 35 minutes or until golden own.

Alice Weller
Bechtelsville, Pennsylvania

HEAVENLY STRAWBERRY DESSERT

ice 1 angel food cake in ½-inch slices and arrange neatly in the bottom of a 9- x 13- x 2-ch pan.

In a medium mixing bowl, combine one 8-ounce package softened cream cheese (at om temperature), 2 cups sifted powdered sugar, and one 8-ounce carton refrigerated hipped topping; mix well to blend. Spread over the cake.

In a small mixing bowl, combine 1½ quarts fresh strawberries with one 16-ounce coniner of strawberry glaze. Spread over the cream cheese mixture. Refrigerate the dessert at ast 4 hours before serving.

Opal Bebee
Anderson, Indiana

JULY

Gladys Taber

Juuly is just plain hot in New England, and there is no use pretending that "this is *most* unusual." It isn't. What is unusual is a cool July, which makes news. It is now corn-growing weather, haying time, ripening time, picnic time. Time to take an early dip in the pond and finish the day with another.

I do enjoy reading all the magazine articles about keeping cool. Evidently many women have time to lie down with pads (dipped in this or that) over their eyes. They relax completely and think cool thoughts; then they take a long, cool bath (with Essence of Alpine in the water). This is followed by a light dusting of Neige de Nuit and the donning of a fresh, flowery frock (pattern number 19405).

I think about these women sometimes as I am making currant jelly. Jelly-making is one of the hottest of summer occupations; for you can-NOT leave it, not at any stage, and lie down with pads over your eyes. You hang over the kettle, and the kitchen is as hot as the Sahara. You have to watch the berries so they won't stick to the kettle. They cook just enough so the juice is extracted, no more, no less. One year I was careless enough to leave wild blackberry jelly while I answered the phone. The jelly went in the glasses all right, but nothing could ever pry it out again. What a difference a few minutes can make!

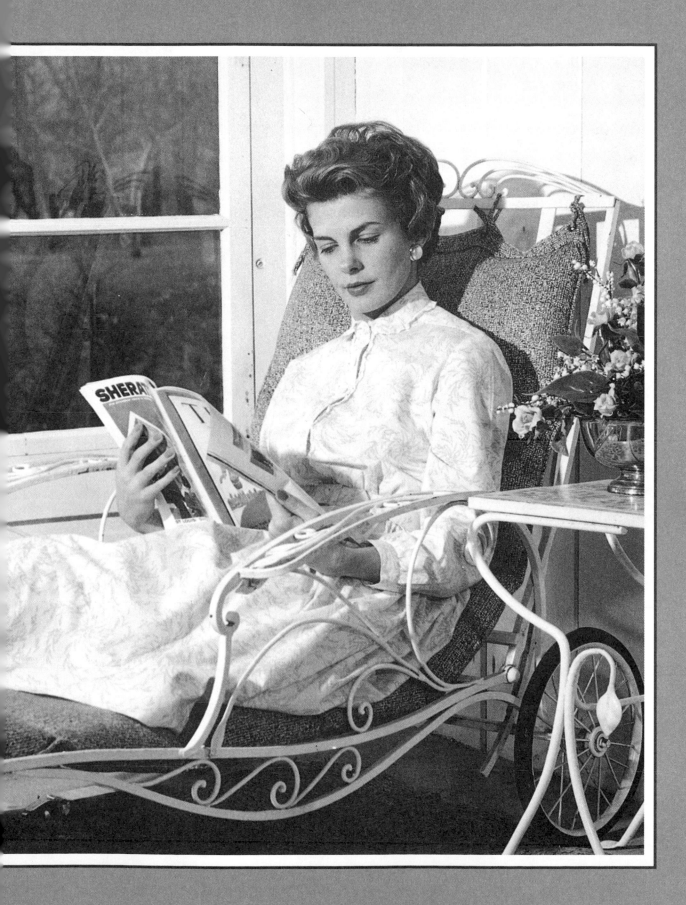

Picnics

Edna Jaques

To picnic on a sun-warmed beach
    Is to bring heaven within reach;
For eating has a special savor
    With wind and sunshine for a flavor,
And tea brewed strong and piping hot
    Is heaven in an earthen pot.

A clean, white beach that circles wide,
    Glistening and salty from the tide,
Seagulls above the white cliffs calling,
    And o'er us golden sunlight falling.
(A sandwich in one hand and tea
    Balance with fear upon your knee.)

A white sail skimming o'er the blue,
    A fisherman whose only crew
Is an old dog—how still he waits
    To watch his master fix the baits.
(Riding the seas in sun and fog,
    A man companioned by a dog.)

So at a picnic we can taste
    The tang of all the tumbling waste
Of seas. The magic of the air,
    Mothers and children everywhere—
All paradise within your reach,
    Eating your supper at the beach.

Bits & Pieces

Never doubt that a small group of thoughtful, committed citizens can change the world. Indeed, it's the only thing that ever has.
MARGARET MEAD

That this nation under God shall have a new birth of freedom and that government of the people, by the people, and for the people shall not perish from the earth.
ABRAHAM LINCOLN

National honor is national property
of the highest value.
JAMES MONROE

I am glad to see that pride in our country
and its accomplishments is not a thing of the
past. I still get a hard-to-define feeling when
the flag goes up, and I know you do too.
Let us hope that none of us loses that feeling.
JOHN H. GLENN

Not for the flag
Of any land because myself was born there
Will I give up my life.
But I will love that land where man is free,
And that will I defend.
EDNA ST. VINCENT MILLAY

For what avail the plough or sail,
Or land or life, if freedom fail?
RALPH WALDO EMERSON

What have you done for liberty?
If nothing, what can freedom mean to you?
WILLIAM JENNINGS BRYAN

Ask not what your country can do
for you—ask what you can do for
your country.
JOHN F. KENNEDY

21

INDEPENDENCE DAY PARADE. Greenport, Long Island, New York. Marty Heitner/Superstock.

THE FLAG GOES BY

Henry Holcomb Bennett

Hats off! Along the street there comes
A blare of bugles, a ruffle of drums,
A flash of color beneath the sky:
Hats off! The flag is passing by!

Blue and crimson and white it shines,
Over the steel-tipped, ordered lines.

Hats off! The colors before us fly,
But more than the flag is passing by.

Days of plenty and years of peace;
March of a strong land's swift increase;
Equal justice, right and law,
Stately honor and reverend awe;

Sign of a nation, great and strong
To ward her people from foreign wrong.
Pride and glory and honor—all
Live in the colors to stand or fall.

Hats off! Along the street there comes
A blare of bugles, a ruffle of drums;
And loyal hearts are beating high.
Hats off! The flag is passing by!

THE PASSENGER CAR. Harold Lambert/Archive Photos.

DAY COACH TO WASHINGTON

When I first found a seat in a coach more than two and a half years ago, the crowds were brash, excited, freshly uniformed, noisy, impatient, and full of loud laughter. Today it is an older crowd, rich in experience, purposeful, relaxed, traveling light, wearing uniforms as casually and comfortably as farmer's denim. War is no longer a hysterical adventure. It is already history with the first phase concluded and the nation turning with terrible but alert assurance to the war against Japan.

Two years ago, I saw a soldier pressed in a corner of the soda counter of Union Station in Washington. Except for a service ribbon, there was nothing unusual about him in that crowd of fresh, unweathered people. But as he turned to move away, he hitched himself up on crutches. He had lost a leg. Then a strange thing happened. The crowd visibly opened before him; laughter along his way broke off. People literally shied away, shocked at this unexpected apparition of the reality of things to come. A year later, within a hundred yards of this first war

casualty, I saw two other casualties, hustling their own bags to the gates. One on crutches was being helped by a vigorous companion, a man of great physical energy and cheerful countenance. They were paratroopers, and the brisk, cheerful one was shifting their bags with two steel hooks where there had been strong hands a few months before. In the surge of weathered and battle-wise soldiers, sailors, and marines, these two got no more than swift, understanding glances. They were confidently on their own.

By choice, I travel by coach. The pontifical atmosphere of a sleek Pullman, with its consciously important passengers who are either stiffly on guard or watching for influential contacts, puts me to sleep; but the lustiness and variety of the crowded coaches are an unfailing stimulant. Here the warm blood of America beats strongly.

After the first hysterical phase of war excitement waned, there came a cold stiffness among the passengers; everyone was fearful of entering into conversation that might betray vital information. At night, window shades were drawn tight as each train left the Pennsylvania Station and rushed south across the flat New Jersey plain. The interiors were gloomy with smoke, and there was little conversation among the slumped figures pressed so closely together. This was in the days of the first convoys. Dark trains moved mysteriously in the night, the limiteds slowed to a stop or crawled hesitatingly at junctions where the troops were moving toward embarkation points, and endless freight trains rumbled to the jumping-off point for the Murmansk run and the African invasion.

By the coming of spring last year, self-conscious citizens and servicemen had acquired sophistication and skepticism. Conversations gradually became easy and general. The trainload was no longer a group of sensitive and suspicious individuals, but rather a family crowd, not greatly concerned with national policies, but tremendously interested in personal affairs. During one of those early trips, there was an unsalted marine who was stimulated by corps traditions and tried to make time with a couple of brittle, young women on their way to Chestnut Hill. His white cap was jaunty, and his approach was brisk and assured, but it got him nowhere. The women simply ignored him with a casual superiority he could not understand. Standing by their seat, he spoke with all-conquering gaiety. Not only did they not hear him, they didn't even see him. In desperation, he appealed to the passengers, "Maybe I'll be flying over Tokyo in a couple of weeks, and they won't even look at me!"

The continuous stream of servicemen is like a broken army in all but spirit—straggling, clustering together, moving in swirling groups of army, navy, and marine uniforms of all ranks and grades, mingling with and almost overwhelming the hurrying civilians with their briefcases and bags, their babies, women, and bundles.

"Hi, mate!" says the sailor.

"Hi, bud!" says the soldier.

"Hi, pop!" says the marine.

But to the girl in uniform, they all say "sister."

I shared a seat with a WAC (Women's Army Corps), a full technical sergeant. She was a handsome, firm woman with an air of kindly competence. She came from Scranton, and she had a calm, even voice that must have inspired loyalty and respect among all who worked with her.

Generally there is little by which to identify or localize individuals or groups on the coach. The uniforms and the wrinkled casualness of traveling outfits leave few clues to location, occupation, income, or social and educational background. Yet the variety of individual characteristics is endless, and nostalgia for the home section is quickly evident after a few minutes of conversation.

I've spent hours talking about the bevel of a plowshare with a New York farmer; of maple bush in Vermont; oyster pirating in the Chesapeake; the pile of arsenic under the big stack at Butte, Montana; the western quarter horse and the Pennsylvania timber topper; Mississippi river boats; the smelt run in the Michigan streams; lumbering on the Olympic Peninsula; and fishing on the gulf.

A young ensign from Boston started me thinking. He didn't like the relatively poor pay of army life and the big wages paid in industry. Why should a soldier get only fifty dollars a month for doing what he does? I said the soldier doesn't work for money; he gives his services for something infinitely more valuable, since you can't put a price on life. He told me his family was well off and he lived in a city. His education had been paid for by his father; his father had also paid for his vacations, his clothing, and his recreation. Without money, he was lost. To my mind, he was one of the most insecure young men I had yet met.

A corporal from Missouri with battle-scarred ribbons told me that since the European war was over, he was going back to the farm. "I've seen a lot," he said, "and I know I can get more money in the city. But, boy, I can get a lot more living on the farm."

All the words, all the books, all the pictures the mind and hands of man have recorded cannot encompass the pageant of the millions pouring and crowding into these cars that are shuttled back and forth at a mile a minute between the great cities of the Atlantic Seaboard. Here is something the world has never known before—a fusion of all nations, of all peoples, not into one typical race, but into one homogeneous congregation united by one political creed—government of the people, by the people, for the people. Here are the people, traveling together.

Reprinted from *The Saturday Evening Post* © June 23, 1945. Written by William Ashley Anderson.

LEGENDARY AMERICANS

NANCY SKARMEAS

BETSY ROSS

The popular legend of Betsy Ross and the American flag was born in the spring of 1870 when Mrs. Ross's grandson, William Canby, presented a paper to the Pennsylvania State Historical Society. His paper told the story of when a secret committee of the Continental Congress visited Canby's grandmother's Philadelphia upholstery shop in 1776. The head of that committee, Canby told his audience, was none other than George Washington, and the group's mission was to design and produce a unique flag for the would-be American nation. They came to see Mrs. Ross because of her reputation as a seamstress. According to Canby, Mrs. Ross so impressed Mr. Washington and his committee with her creativity and sewing skills that they entrusted to her the creation of the very first version of the Stars and Stripes.

Mr. Canby's story—which had been told to him by his Aunt Clarissa, who claimed to have heard it from her mother, Betsy Ross herself—was instantly embraced by historians and the American people. Three years later, the story was repeated in *Harper's Monthly* magazine, and by

1880 Betsy Ross's name and story had been added to the revised edition of George Preble's *Origin and History of the American Flag*. From there it was a small step onto the pages of school textbooks and straight into the hearts and minds of the American people.

By the turn of the century, the Betsy Ross Memorial Association formed to raise funds for creating a museum out of the Philadelphia house where Betsy Ross did her legendary sewing. Contributors to the group's efforts received a miniature print of a painting by Charles H. Weisberger called *Birth of Our Nation's Flag*. The painting depicted Mrs. Ross proudly displaying her completed flag to George Washington and his committee. The legend of Betsy Ross came to life on Weisberger's canvas, which had made its debut a few years earlier at the 1893 Columbian Exposition in Chicago. As the nineteenth century gave way to the twentieth, Betsy Ross's transformation from an anonymous colonial woman to a bona fide American heroine was complete, and William Canby's cherished family tale was an accepted part of American history.

The truth of the matter, however, is that Canby himself had searched for facts to back up his family's oral tradition, but was unable to turn up any solid proof of his grandmother's involvement in the making of the flag. It is a fact that Betsy Ross owned and operated an upholstery shop in Philadelphia, but the only evidence that she had anything at all to do with government flag making is a record of payment made to Mrs. Ross in May of 1777 by the Pennsylvania State Navy Board for the making of "ships colors."

The basic facts of Betsy Ross's life are well-documented. She was born Elizabeth Griscom in Philadelphia in January of 1752, one of seventeen children of Samuel and Rebecca Griscom. Betsy was educated as a Quaker and learned the skills of needlework from her mother. She was married for the first time in 1773 to John Ross, an Anglican. The marriage outside her family's faith led to her expulsion from Quaker society, although she later became a member of the Society of Free Quakers. Shortly after their marriage, John and Betsy Ross began their upholstery business in Philadelphia. When Mr. Ross was killed while serving in the militia in January of 1776, Betsy worked hard to continue the business on her own. In the following years, she married and was widowed two more times and gave birth to seven children. Betsy's second husband, Joseph Ashburn, was captured by the British at sea and eventually died in an English prison. Her third husband, John Claypoole, with whom she had five daughters, died in 1817 after thirty-four years of marriage. Betsy Griscom Ross Ashburn Claypoole died in Philadelphia in 1836 at the age of eighty-four.

Did Betsy Ross design or sew the first American flag? The truth may never be known. It is entirely possible that the committee headed by George Washington brought its design for a flag to the Ross upholstery shop and asked Mrs. Ross to use her needle and thread to make their ideas reality, and it is not unthinkable that some of Mrs. Ross's ideas were incorporated into the flag's design. It is almost certain that whoever did sew that first flag was a woman; if not Betsy Ross, than some other, anonymous, seamstress. In William Canby's version of the story, Mrs. Ross showed Mr. Washington and his committee how to make a five-pointed star with a single cut of the scissors, which impressed them greatly and prompted them to abandon their plans for six-pointed stars in favor of the seamstress's version.

Legend or fact? Perhaps the answer is unimportant. History by its very nature is a blending of facts and records with myth, legend, and lore. Whether Betsy Ross designed the very first Stars and Stripes, whether she translated the ideas of the Continental Congress committee to fabric, or whether she merely sewed ships colors for the navy, she is now a part of our history. Betsy Ross was a strong, independent woman who ran a business and raised a family despite suffering the deaths of three beloved husbands, two of whom were lost in connection to the battle for independence from Great Britain. Her presence adds color, depth, and diversity to the story of America; and even if her story blends fact with fiction, it is, at the very least, a symbolic recognition of the contributions—often behind-the-scenes and unrecognized—of American women to the founding and building of our nation.

TRAVELER'S *Diary*

Michelle Prater Burke

INDEPENDENCE HALL. Philadelphia, Pennsylvania.
Photograph courtesy of Independence National Historical Park.

INDEPENDENCE NATIONAL HISTORICAL PARK
Philadelphia, Pennsylvania

In the last quarter of the eighteenth century, Philadelphia, Pennsylvania, was the center of some of America's most important developments as well as the world's most creative political thought. Within the space of a few square blocks, Independence National Historical Park has preserved the scenes of this early Philadelphia in all its original splendor. No other cluster of buildings and sites conjures up so many images of great personages and significant events associated with the American Revolution and the founding of the nation.

Each year, millions of people interested in gaining a deeper appreciation of the heritage of Amerca visit Independence National Historical Park. The diverse park is rich in attractions—government buildings, restored homes, venerable churches, a portrait gallery, and even an operating eighteenth-century restaurant. A casual stroll through the park will reveal the stunning variety of carefully preserved or reconstructed buildings and sites.

Prominent sites that lure park visitors include the First Bank of the United States, the Army-Navy Museum, and the Benjamin Franklin National Memorial, which honors Philadelphia's most illustrious citizen. Franklin—printer, publisher, statesman, and world-renowned scientist—chose the city as the site for the house and printing office he built during the early years of the American Revolution. The park's Franklin Court features a remarkable sculpture that depicts where these noted buildings once stood and offers a tribute to Franklin's accomplishments.

One of the great treasures of the park is Independence Hall. For many years, the building played a significant role in our nation's founding. From George Washington's appointment as commander in chief of the Continental Army, to the important meeting to decide the design of the American flag, to the adoption of the Articles of Confederation, Independence Hall was the historic site. A fine example of Georgian architecture, the building began as the State House of the Province of Pennsylvania and became the site for the adoption of two of our nation's greatest charters. Within its walls, the Declaration of Independence was adopted in 1776 and the Constitution was written in 1787. The original silver inkstand used to sign both these famous documents remains at Independence Hall to this day.

Another celebrated site in the park is the Liberty Bell. On July 8, 1776, the Liberty Bell was rung in Independence Square to commemorate the first reading of the Declaration of Independence to the citizens of Philadelphia. Since the history of the bell is a combination of facts and folklore, historians are unsure of the exact date the bell acquired its now famous crack. According to tradition, an earlier crack widened irreparably when the bell was last tolled on Washington's birthday in 1846.

Although it tolls no longer, the Liberty Bell retains its vital role as an enduring, world-wide symbol of freedom. Once displayed in Independence Hall, the bell is now housed in the glass-walled Liberty Bell Pavilion to make the bell more accessible to the many people who hope to see and touch this important piece of American history.

While Independence Hall and the Liberty Bell are the best-known treasures of Independence National Historical Park, thousands of noteworthy objects are among the park's extensive holdings. Displayed in fifty-four historic room reconstructions and forty-five separate exhibit areas throughout the park, the wide range of objects includes fine furniture created by Philadelphia artisans that rivals the best of European craftsmen; authentic eighteenth-century china and silver; and words and images on paper and canvas that chronicle the emergence of the American identity.

LIBERTY BELL. Philadelphia, Pennsylvania.
Photograph courtesy of Independence National Historical Park.

The inscription that circumscribes the crown of the Liberty Bell reads, "Proclaim Liberty throughout all the Land unto all the Inhabitants Thereof." It is the spirit and history of this liberty that Independence National Historical Park has successfully preserved for its many visitors to cherish. The park is a true memorial to the momentous decisions and events that established America's independence and that continue to profoundly influence our lives today.

July the Fourth

Evelynn Merilatt Boal

My childhood days afford me
　　Sweet patterns to recall;
Some vivid pictures linger
　　From days when I was small.

July the Fourth was special.
　　I could not wait to write
My name in flaming letters
　　On pages of the night

Or draw an airborne castle
　　Then weep to see it fade,
But glory in the magic
　　Of images I'd made.

And I could bypass bedtime
　　(Sometimes till even ten!)

To watch the Roman candles
　　In skies above our glen.

I'd heard the Declaration
　　Of seventeen seventy-six
But did not know how serious
　　Were wars and politics.

The passing years have proven
　　The price of liberty,
The need for ceaseless efforts
　　To keep our homeland free.

July the Fourth's still special,
　　A day to celebrate
With patriotic fervor
　　What makes our country great.

The Aromas of Travel

Diane Crosby

Something is decidedly different about the way we travel today. Airplanes, tour buses, and other atmospherically controlled vehicles have stolen one of the best parts of a vacation: how things smell.

We are told that scents greatly affect mood and plant themselves forever in our memories. Who can't recall how his or her grandmother's house smelled or the pungent earthiness of a cellar?

Vacation smells were the best. We drove with the windows down in those long ago days because few cars had air conditioning. Even with our eyes closed or at night, we could identify where we were because of the smells. Neighborhoods brought the sweet fragrance of freshly mowed grass. As we passed farms, hay scents wafted in, mixed with the heavy odor of cow fields. The earth called us with the scents of newly plowed soil or onions grown to maturity.

Once my father and I were traveling by night in our '63 Rambler when we were sure we had just driven deep into hog country. The smell hung heavy on our olfactory nerves as we rambled south. The night sky was filled with clouds so dark that we could only imagine the vastness of the hog farm we were riding past. Only when we came upon a town did we discover that we'd been trailing a hog truck for miles.

Still, most aromas were pleasant. Stands of pine, honeysuckle, and gardenias added to the mix. Then the occasional skunk would crinkle our noses.

Smells governed our choice of eating stops. Barbecue was discernible at a distance, as were steaks, hamburgers, and chicken. Our mouths watered before we ever saw the restaurants.

Afternoons approached with that sudden aromatic sensation of rain in the air. We knew it as well as our ABCs. The scent lingered until the skies spilled forth with hard raindrops. As a child, I stole a few moments to dash my hand out of the window and feel the drops that pelted like stones on my palm. Too soon, I'd be admonished to roll up the window. There we sat in muggy heat until the storm passed and we were free to feel the air again. After the rain, the smells changed once more when the steamy aromas of earth and human-made things were brought to life.

A musty waft of saltwater marsh was as much our clue that our destination was at hand as was the sight of palm trees and palmettos. Many find the marsh smell offensive. To me, it evoked days at the beach and lazy nights in a hammock. The salt air of the ocean is different—clean, crisp, renewing. A whiff of that air and I could feel the surf tickling my toes.

City travel demands that we shield ourselves from the fumes of too many cars crammed into too small a space. Safety from many dangers forces us to narrow our environment and maintain its temperature.

But on the road, down the highways of this land, the smells are still there. Fresh fields, flowers in season, a summer's rain—this is God's potpourri.

We block them out now, these aromas of travel. It's a great loss, I think. So as often as I can, I roll down my windows and give my senses a grand vacation.

Handmade Heirloom

Mary Skarmeas

Flags sewn by Connie Meador, Nashville, Tennessee. Jerry Koser Photography.

When Freedom from her mountain height
Unfurled her standard to the air,
She tore the azure robe of night
And set the stars of glory there.

—Joseph Rodman Drake
"The American Flag"

FLAGS FOR HOME

Joseph Rodman Drake's words are thought provoking. Our nation's flag is truly more than just beautiful colors; it is a symbol of national sovereignty, history, and unity. We call upon the Stars and Stripes to express our feelings of joy, pride, sympathy, and mourning. George Washington, commenting on the evolution and symbolism of the Stars and Stripes, stated, "We take the star from the heaven, the red from our mother country, separating it by white stripes, thus showing we have separated from her, and the white stripes shall go down to posterity representing liberty." The power of the flag to unite and inspire is matched by few other symbols.

Although it is not known when the first flag was made or flown, archaeologists believe that flags have been a part of human civilization for more than five thousand years. Historians conjecture that the first flags originated as a means of identification during times of war; from there, as nations emerged and grew, the flag evolved into a full-time national symbol. We Americans—who officially adopted the red, white, and blue of Old Glory on June 14, 1777— fly our flags on many special days, including the Fourth of July, Memorial Day, Veterans Day, and, of course, Flag Day. We sing the flag's praise in the patriotic verses of "You're a Grand Old Flag" and our national anthem, "The Star-Spangled Banner." We fly our flag at schools and churches and post offices and courthouses and on the porches of our own homes; some families faithfully raise the flag each morning and ceremoniously lower it each evening. The flag also has a central role in more solemn occasions—our flags fly at half-mast in honor of our fallen leaders, and the colors gracefully drape the coffins of our servicemen and women as a badge of honor for the fallen and their families.

In recent years, Americans, loyal as always to their national flag, have taken a cue from its symbolic heritage and begun to use personalized flags to create their own unique brand of symbolism. Flags have become a new means of communication. Without those "back-fence" chats that neighbors enjoyed in days gone by, flags help keep us in touch in a different way. As I ride around my town, I see colorful flags of all descriptions flying proudly from front porches. Besides being decorative, the flags can provide insight into the special hobbies and interests of the people who live inside. Judging from the flags in my own neighborhood, I have neighbors who enjoy gardening, sailing, soccer, hot-air ballooning, bird-watching, clowns, and dogs. The flags change with the seasons or holidays and depict such a variety of subject matter that I rarely see duplicates. During the spring, birds and flowers are favored; in the summer, boating and beach scenes prevail; come fall, it is apples, pumpkins, and turkeys; and in the winter, the flag choices truly abound—snowmen, sleighs of toys, Santas, angels, candles, drummer boys, olive branches, and more. The most unique and amusing flag I have yet seen appeared one day during last winter's seemingly endless fury of snowstorms—one of the worst winters we have seen in New England for many years. During February, after the ninth or tenth snowstorm in as many weeks, I spotted a charming flag with a scene of fresh-fallen snow and lacy snowflakes on a sky blue background. The emphatic statement "THAT'S ENOUGH!" was boldly printed across the bottom. This flag made us all

laugh. In the best tradition of the flag, it was a symbol of a people united—against winter!

With flags becoming so popular, it was just a matter of time before creative craftspeople began designing their own; craft stores quickly followed with patterns and fabric to meet the demand. With basic sewing skills, it's easy to make a personalized flag to commemorate special occasions—and what a unique gift! Flags can be made to welcome home a family member who has been away at school or in the service. They can congratulate a bride and groom on a wedding day, wish happy birthday to a friend, or announce a new addition to the family.

Most of the commercial flags that I have seen are made with a strong nylon material, but they can be handmade with any heavy cotton fabric—duck, trigger, sailcloth, canvas—or sport nylon. The flags are constructed so that the same design flies on both sides. The appliqués are cut in pairs, placed on the background fabric, hand-stitched, and then stitched again using a machine satin stitch. Excess fabric is trimmed away close to the stitching on both sides. The patterns provide detailed instructions, and I found salespeople at the craft and sewing stores I visited more than willing to answer questions and give advice. Even if you want to try your hand at a design of your own from the start, invest in a pattern for the general instructions; it will save you time and confusion. Whether from your own design or from a pattern, each one of your handmade flags should be signed and dated; this addition gives a personal touch and bestows heirloom status.

Families still proudly display their nation's colors, but more and more they also use a flag to display their own special colors. In many homes, hanging flags—to commemorate seasons, anniversaries, holidays, births—has become a new family tradition. So often our fondest childhood memories are of the simple, shared rituals of family life. Something as simple as a flag flying from the front porch can be an heirloom, treasured not for its monetary value, but for its symbolic value. Like the very first flags and the flags of the nations of the world, our flags proudly proclaim our identity, or at least one small piece of it. Fly a flag of your own— you will add a splash of color to your home, send a message to all those who pass by, and give the whole family something to smile about.

Mary Skarmeas lives in Danvers, Massachusetts, and is studying for her bachelor's degree in English at Suffolk University. Mother of four and grandmother of one, Mary loves all crafts, especially knitting.

Homespun

Rosa Mary Clausen-Mohr

A piece of homespun in my hand;
My fingers hold it tenderly,
Caressing threads still firm and strong
That blend in patterned harmony.

For years the weaver is at rest;
The noisy shuttle long is still.
The worn-out treadle ne'er replaced
That once obeyed the weaver's will.

Many years have passed and still
The weavings of that life I see
With threads of faith and high ideals,
Like bits of homespun left for me.

"Teach us delight in simple things.

—Rudyard Kipling

Opposite Page HOMESPUN EMBROIDERY. Dianne Dietrich Leis Photography.

THROUGH MY WINDOW

Pamela Kennedy

Art by Russ Flint

RIGHT-BRAIN SEWING

My first formal encounter with a sewing machine was in junior high. I could hardly wait to unlock the secrets of stitchery, to delve into the pattern book's mysteries, to solve the riddles of fashion and form. What I got in Mrs. Browne's seventh-grade home economics class was butcher aprons.

Mrs. Browne believed seams were the sewing equivalent of DNA; they were the building blocks from which all serviceable garments could be constructed. Ever faithful students, we completed graceful curves, straight hems, and tidy, square corners and created aprons that were "productive and practical." Mrs. Browne bundled them up for the Sisters of Mercy in Ghana, and we went on to the cooking unit for baking powder biscuits. Mrs. Browne was not much on frills.

I now appreciate how difficult it is to introduce youngsters to the world of sewing, but I still think Mrs. Browne missed the boat. The Sisters of Mercy notwithstanding, it would have been much more practical to give us a unit on costume design. I've been a mother for years and have yet to be asked to make a butcher apron. On the other hand, someone at my house is always needing a costume.

I'm convinced that hospital maternity wards should pass out costume instructions with every baby, because within a year of its birth each child experiences Halloween. First-time moms seem to approach it as the initial test of their parenting aptitude. I've seen babies in the neighborhood parade encased in tiny dragon outfits complete with stuffed tails and little felt flames or dressed like miniature clowns buried in yards of polka-dot ruffles.

38

While these tots obviously belong to over-achieving mothers with newfangled sewing machines, I tend toward the more simple. My favorite baby costume is the "pumpkin." Put the baby in an orange fabric bag, cinch it snug around the neck, and attach a green paper leaf to baby's head with double stick tape—voilà!

Of course the real challenge comes when children get to elementary school. My offspring all seemed to have teachers who thought dressing the part somehow enhanced learning. These educators obviously were childless and had never stayed up all night making a George Washington wig out of cotton batting or redesigning last year's Grecian goddess costume into something fit for the ghost of Christmas past.

Teachers with backgrounds in English lean toward characters from literature, of course, and social studies teachers like historical figures. At least for these costumes you have some precedents and can look up pictures in books. The problem I have is with this new approach to learning called "whole brain." Despite what my children might think, I have always been an advocate for using the whole brain, but this new idea in education is a bit more complex than just "using your head." As I understand it, left-brained people apparently get focused on facts, numbers, charts, and concrete things while right-brained folks favor the abstract, the artistic, and the creative. (According to my calculations, this makes most of us half-wits, but I don't think that is the proper conclusion to draw from this exciting new area of psychology!)

Anyway, in an effort to utilize the whole brain of each student, my daughter's science teacher recently sent home a note requesting that "your child come to school Tuesday dressed like his/her favorite scientific fact!" Now, I've been making costumes for almost two decades, but even I was stopped by this one. We pulled down the big box of dress-up clothes I had saved through three children. My daughter and I discarded Superman, a fairy princess, Rip Van Winkle, numerous animal outfits, wigs, tiaras, Christmas pageant robes,

and Indian headdresses. Both sides of my brain hurt.

That night at dinner, we put it to the family. The older brothers made numerous suggestions not suitable for elementary school; and my husband, hopelessly left-brained, just kept mumbling, "This whole assignment doesn't make sense!" At that moment, the cat jumped onto the table and bumped into my daughter's arm, thereby propelling a forkful of spaghetti into her lap.

"That's it!" I shouted triumphantly. "Quick, sweetie, stand up!"

My mystified daughter rose to her feet, and we all watched as the glob of spaghetti made its way down the front of her skirt in a bright red trail. I pointed at it with delight and announced, "There's your costume for tomorrow—gravity!"

She had some initial reservations about the idea, but not I. Spurred on by a burst of activity obviously emanating from the right side of my brain, I found an old, white T-shirt and an indelible marker. In bold block letters, I wrote "GRAVITY—IT'S A DOWNER" followed by an arrow aimed at the spaghetti stain on my daughter's skirt.

"This is fantastic!" I crowed.

"This is ridiculous!" the boys declared.

"Are you sure this is what the teacher meant?" inquired my husband.

"Is or is not gravity a scientific fact?" I countered. I could sense victory.

In the morning, my daughter trudged off to school, costume in hand. As she turned the corner, I uttered a little prayer.

"Please, Lord, don't let the math teacher get creative."

Pamela Kennedy is a freelance writer of short stories, articles, essays, and children's books. Wife of a naval officer and mother of three children, she has made her home on both U.S. coasts and currently resides in Honolulu, Hawaii. She draws her material from her own experiences and memories, adding highlights from her imagination to enhance the story.

Readers' Reflections

Summer Fun

Apple blossoms and cherry trees,
  Butterflies and honey bees,
Warm breezes and summer sun—
  Days filled with play and fun.

Dogs barking and cows lowing,
  Grandma baking and gardens growing,
Horseback riding and new-mown hay—
  Carefree days of fun and play.

These are days I like to remember
  From early June until September.
Barefoot, blue jeans, and peasant blouse—
  Summer days at Grandma's house.

Kathleen Lowery
Frankston, Texas

Dreaming of Warmer Places

The ocean is a beautiful place
  Where I have been before.
I'd like to walk again someday
  Along that sandy shore.

The tide brings in rolling waves,
  Sliding over my feet,
And up above the sun shines down
  With such intensive heat.

I'd like to be there every day
  And fill my life with joy,
But unfortunately for me,
  I live in Illinois.

Holly Williams
Chillicothe, Illinois

Country Lanes

There's nothing like a country lane
  Waxed to a shine with Autumn rain,
Or buried deep beneath the glow
  Of moonlight mixed with winter snow,

Or strewn as pretty as you please
  With petals of spring's apple trees,
Unless of course it should be one
  With polka dots of summer sun.

Merry Browne
Louisville, Kentucky

Editor's Note: Readers are invited to submit unpublished, original poetry for possible publication in future issues of Ideals. *Please send copies only; manuscripts will not be returned. Writers receive $10 for each published submission. Send material to Read-ers' Reflections, Ideals Publications Inc., 535 Metroplex Drive, Suite 250, Nashville, Tennessee 37211.*

The Lightning Bug

When I see a lightning bug,
   I often wonder why
He blinks his lights on and off
   As he goes flying by.

It certainly would seem better,
   And safer for him too,
If he would just leave his light on
   The whole night through.

Does he have to blink his light
   Like the turn signal on a car
So other bugs can see him coming
   From way off afar?

Or is he using a kind of code
   To speak with all his friends,
To tell them all the news
   As the day comes to an end?

Well, it sure seems funny to me;
   But whatever the reason,
Does he charge his battery in winter
   For the coming summer season?

Diana Meschberger
Auburn, Indiana

The Mountain

The mountain is majestic
   As it reaches to the sky;
At times it seems to bow its head
   To let the clouds go by.

The sun in all its glory
   Peeks o'er its jaded crests
While the birds declare their domicile
   And snuggle in their nests.

The rippling of the clear cool stream
   Is music to my ears.
The tiny pebbles look like gems
   Polished by the years.

The mountain is a monument
   To those who there have trod,
And no other thing can quite compare
   To this masterpiece of God.

Bernice Huber
Lake Worth, Florida

COLLECTOR'S CORNER

Lisa C. Thompson

SAMPLER CREATED BY REBECCA MORRIS, 1787. Shelburne Museum, Shelburne, Vermont.
Photograph by Ken Burris.

ANTIQUE SAMPLERS

Antique samplers provide collectors not only with a tangible piece of feminine history but also an intimate look into the personal life of the seamstress herself. As young girls practiced their stitching skills, they invariably included reflections of their own lives in the details of their work. Along with the typical alphabet, numerals, and flower borders on her carefully-worked sampler, the seamstress would often include a stitched pic-ture of her own home, a public building in her town, or her church. These personal touches are often what motivate collectors to buy.

While collectors love the sampler today for its beautiful embroidery and historical charm, the sampler originated as a substitute for expensive pattern books as well as a canvas on which young fingers practiced intricate stitches. The word *sampler* is derived from the Latin word *exemplar*. This is why samplers were often worked in any number of different stitches. The stitches provided examples to the seamstress when she later married and embroidered her own linens.

Girls as young as six years old have stitched samplers in England since the Middle Ages. The practice gained popularity through the years and by the sixteenth and seventeenth centuries was commonplace throughout England and many European countries. The women who voyaged to the New World brought their samplers with them and taught the skills to their daughters. The sampler of one of these women, Loara Standish, daughter of Captain Miles Standish of Plymouth, is on display at the Pilgrim Hall Museum in Plymouth, Massachusetts. It is undated but known to have been stitched before 1656. Loara's sampler is long and narrow, typical of the time, because the loom on which the linen was woven was narrow. Stitched in blues and browns, Loara's intricate work is one of the earliest surviving examples of an American-made sampler.

By the eighteenth century, all young women were expected to be accomplished in the latest embroidery techniques. Finishing schools boasted of their embroidery lessons, and wealthier families hired skilled tutors to teach their daughters the mysteries of the needle. The teacher often devised the pattern and instructed her students to copy it with little variation. This is evident among some of the samplers from the same region that resemble each other noticeably. Several different kinds of sampler styles were taught then and are collected today. They include alphabet samplers; pictorial samplers, which combined painting and stitching; mending and darning samplers; and map, or geographical, samplers. Map samplers were especially popular in England and to a lesser extent in the United States. Another sampler style is the genealogical sampler, which detailed family records and was particularly popular in the United States.

SAMPLERS
John Drinkwater

He errs who thinks those hands were set
All spinster-like and cold
Who spelt a scarlet alphabet
And birds of blue and gold
And made immortal garden plots
Of daisies and forget-me-nots.
The bodkins wove an even pace;
Yet these are lyrics too,
Breathing of spectral lawn and lace,
Old ardors to renew;
For in the corners Love would keep
His fold among the little sheep.

Samplers were worked on a variety of foundation fabrics, including plain-weave linen, cotton, and wool. Beginning students usually stitched on fabric of loose density, thereby making it easier to count stitches. Samplers stitched on an extremely dense weave wherein it was impossible to count stitches were no doubt completed by accomplished seamstresses.

By the latter nineteenth century, the role of the sampler had gradually shifted from that of an educational tool and pattern book replacement to a leisure-time craft. As the sampler's domestic importance declined, so did its quality. During the 1920s, simple, mail-order patterns offered housewives the opportunity to cross-stitch an easy design quickly. These mail-order patterns usually featured mottoes such as "The world is so full of a number of things, I'm sure we should all be as happy as kings." The monetary value of many of these modern, cross-stitched mottoes is negligible.

The value of a particular sampler is usually determined by complexity of stitch used (crewel stitching is pricier than cross-stitching), intricateness of the pattern, condition of the linen, variety of colors used, and even the overall size of the work. The customary name and date on antique samplers can sometimes offer genealogical clues as to the seamstress's origins, which could possibly increase the historical significance of the piece and therefore its collectible value. Some samplers may be purchased for purely sentimental reasons. For example, a collector may find a sampler bearing the name of the collector's hometown, Christian name, or favorite Bible verse. These treasures of the past can be found at estate sales, antique shops, and even flea markets.

What were once the diligent trials of a schoolgirl's education are now treasured collectibles. Collectors agree that antique samplers offer a charming way to own a piece of history as well as grace your walls with beautiful embroidery.

The County Fair

Jean Mickle

Mother donned her Gibson blouse
   And Father tied his tie.
The entries then were gathered up—
   A patchwork quilt and pie.

Soon they called to hurry us,
   "Come now or we'll be late!
If Mother's entries are not in,
   The judges just won't wait!"

From a distance we could see
    The tents with flags on high.
And once we passed the iron gates,
    We smelled the catfish fry,

Drank lemonade in frothy cups,
    Ate peanuts by the peck.
Dear Mother warned of scary rides,
    "You're sure to break your neck!"

The judging done, we held our breath
    While ribbons were passed out.
If Mother won, (quite modestly)
    We'd clap our hands and shout.

Everyone we knew and loved
    Was sure to gather there.
Who can forget the atmosphere
    Of old-time county fairs?

FOR THE CHILDREN
ARTWORK BY RUSS FLINT

BAREFOOT DAYS
Rachel Field

In the morning, very early,
    That's the time I love to go
Barefoot where the fern grows curly
    And grass is cool between each toe!
On a summer morning-Oh!
On a summer morning.

That is when the birds go by
    Up the sunny slopes of air,
And each rose has a butterfly
    Or a golden bee to wear.
And I am glad in every toe—
Such a summer morning-Oh!
Such a summer morning.

The unique perspective of Russ Flint's artistic style has made him a favorite of Ideals *readers for many years. A resident of California and father of four, Russ Flint has illustrated a children's Bible and many other books.*

Daisies in the Grass

Hazel Adell Jackson

They nod their gleaming, fringy heads—
The daisies in the grass.
They give a glad good-morning
To the children as they pass.
They lift their smiling faces high;
And as the Sun looks down,
He sees his own reflection
In the daisies' tiny crowns.

All day their jaunty heads they toss
As winds of summer blow
And white against the hilltop
Seem a bank of purest snow.

All day with faces fair, upturned,
They polka-dot the leas;
And children tired of playing
Weave white chains beneath the trees.

Deep-set amid the meadow grass
With leaves like tiny spears,
The daisy goes on smiling,
For there's nothing that she fears.
And when the Sun is sinking low,
And weary daisies nod,
Perhaps they're folding tiny hands
To say their thanks to God.

Daisies in the Meadow

Frank Dempster Sherman

At evening when I go to bed,
I see the stars shine overhead;
They are the little daisies white
That dot the meadow of the night.

And often while I'm dreaming so,
Across the sky the moon will go;
It is a lady, sweet and fair,
Who comes to gather daisies there.

For when at morning I arise,
There's not a star left in the skies;
She's picked them all and dropped them down
Into the meadows of the town.

"There grew pied windflowers and violets,
Daisies—those pearled Arcturi of the earth;
The constellated flower that never sets."

—Percy Bysshe Shelley

A SLICE OF LIFE

— Edgar A. Guest —

BIRD NESTS

What a wonder world it is
　For a little girl of five
At the June time of the year
　And so good to be alive
With the meadows to explore,
　Seeking bird nests near and far,
And a dad of forty-four
　Who can show her where they are!

Every evening after tea
　We go wandering about
To the nests which we have found
　Where the little birds are out.
And we tiptoe hand in hand
　To a certain lovely crest
Where delightedly we stand
　At a killdeer's curious nest.

And a meadowlark we know
    With five babies of her own!
What a wonder world it is,
    And what miracles are shown!
She can scarcely stay for tea—
    How she bolts her pudding through—
With so much she wants to see
    And so much she wants to do!

So we hurry out of doors,
    And excitedly we race
To the mother meadowlark
    And the killdeer's secret place.
And we talk of God Who made
    All the birds and trees and flowers,
And we whisper, half afraid,
    "What a wonder world is ours."

Edgar A. Guest began his illustrious career in 1895 at the age of fourteen when his work first appeared in the Detroit Free Press. *His column was syndicated in over 300 newspapers, and he became known as "The Poet of the People."*

A Scrapbook for Dad

Laurie Dawson Wilcox

I open a page in my faded scrapbook,
And there tucked away in a special nook
Is a problem you worked with patience and care;
I remember the night I placed it there.

I see in my scrapbook a ribbon of blue,
A faded corsage with a message from you.

You sent it with love for my graduation;
I wore it with pride and much admiration.

And here in the back is a menu so fine;
You remembered my birthday and took me to dine.
You gave me so much to make my heart glad!
Each page that I turn, I remember you, Dad.

Dad of Mine

Becky Jennings

Time has left its mark on him
In a very tender way;
His shoulders are a little bent,
His hair a little gray.

His eyes are kind and gentle,
And they're dimmed by passing years;

For deep compassion dwells there and
A thousand unshed tears.

Hands that do the best of deeds,
Feet that trod a path divine,
God bless him now and always—
That precious dad of mine.

GRANDPA'S TREE

Lon Myruski

Amid our sprawling meadow
   Stands a lofty cottonwood,
Sturdy, staunch, and steadfast,
   Despite the years it's stood.
Bespreading boughs wave proudly
   Like banners in the breeze,
The guidon of our farmstead—
   We call it Grandpa's tree.

Once underneath its branches
   As soft moonlight bathed the land,
Grandpa, touched by young love,
   Asked Grandma for her hand.
They grew in love together;
   They'd till and hoe and seed,
Then Grandma'd bring a basket—
   They'd lunch 'neath Grandpa's tree.

And as the years ebbed onward,
   How I'd toil at Father's side,
Reaping satisfaction
   From work done with family pride.
Then we'd ride our old Ford tractor
   Out 'cross the grassy sea
To sip the jug of water
   Kept cool 'neath Grandpa's tree.

That cottonwood's still standing
   Although some of us are gone,
And my heart is the haven
   Where those yesterdays live on.
And sometimes close to sundown
   In sunset reverie,
I reach to touch old mem'ries
   That rest 'neath Grandpa's tree.

Opposite Page
COTTONWOOD IN YOSEMITE VALLEY
Yosemite National Park, California
Jeff Gnass Photography

Swimming with Dad

D. A. Hoover

It was August, and we were busy
In the midst of a crop of hay
From dawn to dark, but we never found
Enough time in the day.

How well I remember that blazing noon
With the sun bright overhead.
We ate and rested then rose to go,
But instead my father said,

"The horses should rest a little more,"
(Being thoughtful was just like him)
"Why don't we kill a little time
Down there at the creek and swim?"

Green willows leaned by the swimming hole;
Dragonflies went sailing by
While great, white, cloud-like, mighty towers
Rolled up in the summer sky.

We splashed and swam and floated and cooled—
What a wonderful time we had;
And we talked for days of that special noon,
Out swimming with our dad!

We Dads

R. Armistead Grady

I used to be, some years ago,
Addressed in tones caressing, low,
By such fair names as *Sweetheart, Dear,*
By my fond wife as I drew near.
And *Darling* too, *My Love* also,
I answered to some years ago.

But now, since Jim, Sam, Frank, and Joan
Arrived, I'm just called on the phone.
Called at night, called in the morning,
Sometimes "called" just as a warning.
Addressed as *Say, Listen,* and *Here,*
Seldom, except by proxy, *Dear.*

But what's the difference, for you see,
These children are a part of me.
And all the love my wife bestows
On each of them, she knows o'erflows
To me; and I get my fair part
All filtered through a child's heart.

A TRIBUTE TO

Dad

LaVerne P. Larson

Dad, you are mighty special
Each day of every year.
You truly bless our lives,
And we always hold you dear.

Your words have truth and wisdom.
You're firm, yet gentle too.
Hope and faith and knowledge
Are typical of you.

You strive for higher goals with
A quiet, steady aim.
You're modest when you win;
If you lose, you don't complain.

With respect and admiration
And pride and love, we say,
Dad, our humble thanks to you.
You're a great man every day!

CALIFORNIA CHENIN BLANC WINE GRAPES. Ed Cooper Photography.

JUNE ARBORS

I had a grape arbor at my former home in a small town near Albany and Schenectady, New York. The grapes were small and seedy; and while they made a nice jelly to accompany a tart, I left them each year for the robins who were gathering in flocks for their fall migration. The robins came every summer without fail with their chirps and songs. I enjoyed their liveliness when they were close at hand, and I could watch and hear their ruckus far off in the wild grape thickets at the edge of the woods.

The grape arbor near my home covered a part of the stone walk that led from my house to the well. How often on hot summer days I lingered beneath the arbor with its bowers yielding cool and comfortable shade! Through its gifts of fruit and soothing shade, the arbor offered a refuge to the chirping birds and a resting gardener.

Recently, on a June day of particularly intense heat and sun, I was reminded of the soothing qualities of arbors as my friend Hilda and I were returning to her village after a tour of the Carolina countryside in the foothills of the Blue Ridge Mountains. As we drove down one of the main streets of her town, my friend commented on the comfort that the giant trees gave her as the branches on one side reached over the avenue to mingle with the boughs on the opposite side. Hilda called it a quiet bower, an arbor of soothing calmness. I thought of those tree boughs as arms of comfort in an embrace of loyalty and friendship, an embrace of kindness and compassion, steadfast and sure.

It is no surprise that nature would choose the month of June to remind us of the comfort and unity with which God has surrounded us all.

The author of two published books, Lansing Christman has been contributing to Ideals *for over twenty years. Mr. Christman has also been published in several American, foreign, and braille anthologies. He lives in rural South Carolina.*

Country Church

D. A. Hoover

This is the church where you and I
Once worshiped long ago.
Your hair was gold, and mine was dark;
Now both are streaked with snow.

The bluebells gently wave again,
And happy songsters sing;
But I can see how passing time
Has mellowed everything.

I like to think about you then
So close beside me where
Our hearts and thoughts would lift and thank
The Lord in earnest prayer.

The stained-glass windows are the same;
The golden sun shines through
And makes a rainbow of the place
Where I now sit with you.

These beautiful reflections bring
A warm and loving glow
Because you're here beside me now
As in the long ago.

COUNTRY CHURCH
Wisconsin
Superstock

Noon Woods

Maude Noel

I lay on a soft, verdant bed of sweet clover
    With my head on a pillow of moss.
It was cool and so sweet in my leafy retreat
    With a soft breeze ablowing across.

I dropped all my cares in the brook at my side,
    The ones that return with each day;
And I watched with a smile for just a short while
    As they rippled and rippled away.

Then the last one was gone and the brook hurried on,
    Murmuring, busy, serene;
And I lifted my eyes with a prayer to the skies—
    Bits of blue through the flickering green.

The soft humming sound of the trees all around
    Met the green and gold fragrance of noon.
For a while it was mine, and with sweet peace divine,
    I avowed it was heaven in June!

FOREST GREENERY
Antrim, Pennsylvania
Josiah Davidson Scenic Photography

When Strawberries Flower in the Valley

Loise Pinkerton Fritz

When strawberries flower in the valley
And the roses all bloom, every one,
It is then I recall blue-eyed Sally
With tresses of strawberry blond.

How we'd sit 'neath the rose-covered arbor
When we were but waist-high at best;
I'd pick a red rose, give it to her
To wear on her pink cotton dress.

We'd walk through the fields with our dollies
And gather wild strawberries sweet;
Beside us stayed Laddie, our collie,
Who shared in this summertime treat.

When strawberries flower in the valley
And the roses are fully in bloom,
I remember my childhood friend Sally,
Choice rose of a long-ago June.

From My Garden Journal

by Deana Deck

HONEYSUCKLE

When I was a child, my family lived for a time in Georgia and then spent several years in Virginia. These early years of southern living had a lasting effect on me, partly because in each place I remember backyard walls and fences draped with sweet-smelling honeysuckle. Being a dreamer by nature, one of my favorite pastimes was lying on my back on the freshly mowed lawn, sipping nectar from honeysuckle blossoms, and watching the clouds drift by. At night we slept with the windows open since we had no air conditioners, and all summer I fell asleep enveloped in the rich aroma of honeysuckle. To me, summer and the fragrance of honeysuckle are still synonymous.

When I moved back to the South later in life, one of the things that I was looking forward to was having my own little patch of honeysuckle. When I sought to purchase a vine or two of my own, I was met by looks of disbelief from various garden-center personnel. I quickly discovered that here in the mid-South honeysuckle is considered a scourge, second only to the infamous, much-despised kudzu vine.

Honeysuckle earned an unwelcome reputation after it was planted in the 1930s and 1940s to control erosion and quickly overtook thousands of acres of southern woodland and roadsides. This type is usually the Halliana (*Lonicera japonica*), also known as Japanese or Hall's honeysuckle. Avoid it. Even though you might take great care not to let it get out of control, you cannot keep the birds from eating its attractive, tasty fruit and dropping the seeds far and wide.

That caveat should not limit your options, however. There are hundreds of varieties of honeysuckle, many of them shrub varieties that make nice hedges, but my favorite is vine plants. Several of the best known varieties are recommended by the National Arboretum's *Book of Outstanding Garden Plants* and can be safely planted without danger of infesting the neighborhood with rampant vines.

Honeysuckle can be grown in nearly every state in the Union and has been cultivated for hundreds of years. Remember that scene in Shakespeare's *A Midsummer Night's Dream* in which Oberon speaks of "luscious woodbine"? Woodbine is a honeysuckle species native to the British Isles. It grows well in the United States throughout the South and up through the Pacific Coast, Midwest, and New England and can reach about eight feet.

Honeysuckle is basically a woodland vine, so it always does best if its roots are in a cool, shaded location, even though the vine itself will climb up and bask happily in the hot noonday sun. In his book *Climbers and Wall Plants*, Peter Q. Rose, a well-known British horticulturist, suggests that woodbine is at its best in wild gar-

HONEYSUCKLE

dens or when planted in the shade of ancient oaks. For plantings nearer the house, along walls or fences, or on trellises, Rose suggests the cultivar Belgica, also known as the Early Dutch honeysuckle, which blooms in May and June. Plant it as a companion to the Late Dutch variety Serotina, and you'll enjoy continuous bloom from late spring until the end of July. The fragrant blooms of both these varieties are reddish purple and change to a rich buff-yellow with age.

A somewhat less hardy woodbine, the Italian woodbine (*L. caprifolium*) blooms from late spring through the summer and is also highly fragrant. A plant often found in old estate gardens, *L. x americana* is the result of a cross between *L. caprifolium* and the Mediterranean *L. etrusca* made before 1750. It is quite fragrant and tends to be evergreen in warm climates. Even though it is an old plant, it is still available from nurseries that specialize in woody vines.

One of the more attractive honeysuckles, though not a very fragrant one, is the trumpet honeysuckle, *L. sempervirens*. This plant is native to the eastern United States and in spite of its lack of fragrance is popular for its red, trumpet-shaped blooms and its ability to attract hordes of hummingbirds in summer. This variety is hardy to mostly northern states.

Honeysuckle has few natural enemies and falls victim to no diseases other than leaf curl, which is controlled with dormant sprays of fungicide. It may develop canker or crown gall, which can be cut out. Some plants will develop powdery mildew in hot, damp conditions, but this condition can also be controlled with fungicides or with a solution of baking soda and water.

Honeysuckle vines will benefit from an occasional pruning. If left to their own devices, the vines will climb as high as possible. If the vines are kept trimmed to a manageable six- or eight-foot height, the blooms are more visible and the plant has thicker, glossy, green foliage.

Most of the red-blooming honeysuckles lack the fragrance of the yellow and white varieties. One exception is the lovely Everblooming Honeysuckle, *L. x heckrottii*. This is a hybrid between Koch (*L. americana*), a hybrid itself, and the trumpet honeysuckle, *L. sempervirens*. This fortuitous cross has produced one of the best garden forms of the honeysuckle family. Hardy in mostly northern states, the flowers of the Everblooming Honeysuckle start out a brilliant carmine color, then open to reveal yellow interiors that eventually change to pink. All three colors can be present simultaneously to create a glorious display.

If you start your honeysuckle plantings with a few different varieties, you can soon have a fence or garden wall thickly covered with a variety of blossoms. The fragrant white and yellow blossoms will more than compensate for the lack of fragrance in the more dramatic red varieties. Honeysuckle is an excellent choice of flowering plant to place near a deck or patio where you spend long, leisurely hours on summer evenings.

Once you have several vigorous plants growing, you can propagate more simply by taking cuttings of half-ripened wood in July. Dust the cuttings with rooting hormone and insert them into sandy compost until they root. The rooted cuttings can be set out in the fall in mild climates or carried over indoors or in a cold frame until spring in colder climates.

With its hardy nature and the abundance of stunning varieties, honeysuckle makes a welcome addition to your home's summer surroundings. Its distinct beauty and fragrance will please your senses, and honeysuckle will quickly become a special part of all your summer memories.

Deana Deck lives in Nashville, Tennessee, where her popular garden column is a regular feature in The Tennessean.

My Shepherd Walks Near

Kay Hoffman

The Lord is my Shepherd;
  He ever walks near
To guide and protect me
  Each day of the year.

Beside the still waters,
  Through meadows so fair,
On life's troubled pathways
  I'm safe in His care.

His rod and His staff
  Reassure me anew.
No hills are too steep,
  For He's walking there too,

E'er preparing a table
  With gifts from above
And binding my wounds up
  With His tender love.

Through all of my days
  No more harm will I fear;
It comforts me knowing
  My Shepherd walks near.

WILD MUSTARD AND LUPINE
California
Jeff Gnass Photography

Serenity

Lucille Kleist Shaw

The fish poles lean against the tree;
The boat rests in the bay.
It's time to reminisce about
The joys that made this day.

There's nothing quite as peaceful as
A rosy-tinted lake
With rippling rings and shadows caused
By fishes and their wake.

The orange flames dance gaily round
A knotted branch of oak
As mournful whippoorwills sing low
To beckon all their folk.

The watching stars blink gently as
The shady smoke grows tall.
The blest hours round a warm campfire
Are the nicest hours of all.

Come Walk with Me

Freda V. Fisher

Come walk with me along the hills,
 Among the trees and vines,
Upon a wooded mountain trail,
 Among the firs and pines

Where hemlock dangle lacy arms
 And cedars drape their shawl,
Where deer and cougar gently tread
 And tiny creatures crawl.

We'll walk 'neath shady, leafy bowers
 And climb some sunny peak
To find the very heart of God
 Our souls with longing seek.

Morning

Emily Dickinson

Will there really be a morning?
 Is there such a thing as day?
Could I see it from the mountains
 If I were as tall as they?

Has it feet like waterlilies?
 Has it feathers like a bird?
Is it brought from famous countries
 Of which I have never heard?

Oh, some scholar! Oh, some sailor!
 Oh, some wise man from the skies!
Please to tell a little pilgrim
 Where the place called morning lies.

Peaceful Benediction

Marjorie Fehl Brubaker

Lord, how I need the quiet
    of a summer eve
When heav'n bends low
    to catch the tumult
    of the teeming hours
And cups them in
    the stillness of a placid time
When birds sing softly
And a myriad of stars shine forth
    in peaceful benediction.

FELINE TRANQUILITY
Garden of Native Wildflowers
Missouri
Gay Bumgarner

Readers' Forum

Meet Our Ideals Readers and Their Families

ATTENTION IDEALS READERS: The *Ideals* editors are looking for "favorite memories" for the magazine. Please send a typed description of your favorite holiday memory or family tradition to: Favorite Memories, c/o Editorial Department, Ideals Publications Inc., 535 Metroplex Drive, Suite 250, Nashville, Tennessee 37211.

CAROL PORTER of Westmont, Illinois, sent us this photo of her grandson Bradley, age two, relaxing with some friendly ducks by a pond in a nearby park. Grandma tells us that Bradley is a very active little boy, but here he is taking a break to do some "serious fishing." Bradley loves to play basketball and will soon be showing his one-year-old baby brother how to play! Grandma and Grandpa (Robert) live only two towns away, so visits are frequent. As Carol says, "He brings much happiness to our lives."

THANK YOU Carol Porter and Susan Hosler for sharing with *Ideals*. We hope to hear from other readers who would like to share photos and stories with the *Ideals* family. Please include a self-addressed, stamped envelope if you would like the photographs returned. Keep your original photographs for safekeeping and send duplicate photos along with your name, address, and telephone number to:

READERS' FORUM
IDEALS PUBLICATIONS INC.
535 METROPLEX DRIVE, SUITE 250
NASHVILLE, TENNESSEE 37211

ideals

Publisher, Patricia A. Pingry
Editor, Lisa C. Thompson
Copy Editor, Michelle Prater Burke
Electronic Prepress Manager,
    Amilyn K. Lanning
Editorial Intern, Heather R. McArthur
Contributing Editors, Lansing Christman,
Deana Deck, Russ Flint, Pamela
Kennedy, Patrick McRae, Mary Skarmeas,
Nancy Skarmeas

ACKNOWLEDGMENTS

DAY COACH TO WASHINGTON by William Ashley Anderson reprinted from *The Saturday Evening Post*, copyright © 1945. BAREFOOT DAYS, copyright © 1926 by Doubleday, from *TAXIS AND TOADSTOOLS* by Rachel Field. Used by permission of Doubleday, a division of Bantam Doubleday Dell Publishing Group, Inc. BIRD NESTS from *HARBOR LIGHTS OF HOME* by Edgar A. Guest, copyright © 1928 by The Reilly & Lee Co., used by permission of the author's estate. PICNICS from *DREAMS IN YOUR HEART* by Edna Jaques, published in Canada by Thomas Allen & Son Limited. JULY from *THE STILLMEADOW ROAD* by Gladys Taber, copyright © 1962 by Gladys Taber, copyright re-newed © 1990 by Constance Taber Colby. Reprinted by permission of Brandt & Brandt Literary Agents, Inc. Our sincere thanks to the following author whom we were unable to contact: R. Armistead Grady for WE DADS.

When her mother snapped this photograph, Cassie, age five, was busy playing "mom" with her baby sister, Taylor, age four months. Proud grandmother SUSAN HOSLER of Rives Junction, Michigan, sent us this picture of her two granddaughters. The picture was taken in the girls' backyard last summer. They live only one mile from their grandparents on a country farm with several cats. "Stubby," aptly named for its signature short tail, is shown here vying for the girls' attention.

In the Country

Sandra L. Barnes

Echoes through the hills do roam,
Traveling to some distant home,
Vanish in the vast unknown,
    Each day in the country.

Checkered fields of fruit and grain,
Running wild across the plain,
Rising up through sun, through rain,
    Nurtured in the country.

Breezes dance with calm and grace,
Pause, and gently brush the face,

Flowing to some peaceful place,
    A haven in the country.

Carols end and birds take flight,
Join other creatures in the night,
And take a well-deserved respite
    At evening in the country.

Stillness covers all the land;
Nature rests, both soil and sand,
Sweetly lulled by God's right hand
    At sunset in the country.